T0016111

THE
GHOSTLY TALES
OF
SARATOGA

Published by Arcadia Children's Books
A Division of Arcadia Publishing
Charleston, SC
www.arcadiapublishing.com

Spooky America is a trademark of Arcadia Publishing, Inc.

First published 2022

Manufactured in the United States

ISBN 978-1-4671-9867-7

Library of Congress Control Number: 2022932057

Spooky America

THE
GHOSTLY TALES
OF
SARATOGA

KATE BYRNE

Adapted from *Supernatural Saratoga* by Mason Winfield

arcadia
CHILDREN'S BOOKS

NEW YORK

VT

MA

CT

* ALBANY

SARATOGA

# Table of Contents & Map Key

**Geyser Creek**

# Introduction

Welcome to Saratoga Springs, America's "Spa City"! This is a truly special place. Throughout the years, nations have fought here. Tourists have vacationed here. Local people have worked to keep the area's rich heritage alive. With so much history, it's not much of a surprise that Saratoga is positively gushing with the spirits of the past.

The Iroquois who lived here for centuries believed that the Orenda—the name of a spring at Saratoga Spa State Park—had a kind of mystical life energy to it. Could that explain why the water is believed to have healing powers? When word got out about this very special water, Saratoga Springs became the destination for the well-to-do on the East Coast. The elegant Saratoga Spa (now a state park) was built. The fountains and bathhouses here were modeled after the great spas of Europe. There was an upscale hotel, theaters, and a casino. There were wooded walking paths, reflecting pools, and tree-lined avenues. Truly, it was a luxury spa. No wonder so many ghosts decided to stay here!

That's right—the former citizens of Saratoga Springs mingle with the current ones in many places all over town. They float down the hallways of museums and mansions. They hover in the mist around the town's famed springs. They appear in photographs. Some even attend parties! The supernatural happenings here aren't limited to ghosts, though. Mysterious orbs of light are frequently seen in the area. And if you believe in local legends, there might be some more sinister forces at play here, too. In the past, witches and wizards were said to move about. There were even sightings of strange, shape-shifting creatures that you wouldn't want to meet on a dark, stormy night.

Don't be alarmed. These are just stories... or are they? You'll have to keep reading and decide for yourself. Is Saratoga a charming small town with a rich past, or a hub of supernatural activity? Or both? Either way, get ready to learn more about the Saratoga's spookier side!

# Spirited Springs

The mineral springs of Saratoga put it on the map as a tourist destination. People believed that if they could bathe in or drink the water from these sources, their health problems would disappear. Later, some businesspeople got the idea that they could bottle this famous water and sell it. That way, people everywhere could benefit from it, even if they couldn't come here for a visit. With that, the local soda water industry was born! Everyone seems to agree that there is something very special about the water around here. Some people believe the water contains the magical powers of the supernatural spirits that live inside it. According to local legends, the springs you find around here are home to "little people"—a kind of water spirit or fairy.

Imagine you are walking in the forest near a rushing creek. You see a big flat stone in the middle of the water. It's so delightful, it looks like a scene from a fairytale. Or perhaps your walk takes you to a misty waterfall. It looks like something magical could happen here! If the stories are true, these scenic places probably really are enchanted! Spots like this are known in folklore as "little people places." The Mohawk people believed in a type of little person called

a "stone-thrower." Stone-throwers were said to live in local rivers, lakes, and springs. They oversaw the caretaking of these places.

A French priest who visited the area in the 1600s recorded what he knew about the stone-throwers. When arriving on the rocky shore of a local lake, his Mohawk travel companions became very quiet and serious. They walked along the beach picking up small pieces of flint. These were gifts from the stone-throwers in the water, they told him. In exchange, they left tobacco for the little people. With this exchange of gifts, they would be protected and the little people would be happy. The stone-throwers were not great to look at according to stories. They had skinny, fish-like faces. Sometimes local people still report seeing

them. They are said to row around in stone canoes. If you happen to be near a stream or lake, keep a lookout for them.

One place, Kateri Spring near Fultonville, is said to be visited by a different kind of spirit. A Mohawk woman named Kateri Tekakwitha was baptized here in the Catholic tradition. She was later known to perform miracles. She was the first Native American to be honored as a Catholic saint. Although she died many years ago, some say they still see her near the spring. Seeing her is thought to be a sign of a blessing.

If you visit Saratoga Springs Spa Park, you may encounter a spirit you may have heard about before. Visitors have long reported seeing a "Woman in White" apparition near the water. That's a common kind of ghost—a wispy, floating female apparition dressed all in white. This kind of spirit has been seen at several different pools and water features in the park. Is it all the same spirit or are there women in white all over the park? Or could it just be a trick of the light on the water and the mist?

When you are in the park, you'll certainly see the Lincoln Baths, a grand, imposing bathhouse with Corinthian columns. It's impressive, and it's haunted! New employees are warned by those who have been there for some time to be prepared for strange happenings there.

But not all the spirits in the park linger near the water. There is a strange phenomenon that happens to people walking on the park's many trails and pathways. Observers report seeing what looks like a figure walking slowly off in the distance. But no matter how fast the person walks, the figure is always in the same position on the horizon. You can't get closer to the figure, and it never seems to move.

----

Most, if not all, old theaters are haunted. The Spa Little Theater is no exception. There are several ideas about who might be haunting its storied halls. Some say it's an actor called Monty Woolley who performed in the theater many times. He was known as a versatile character actor, but also for his strongest identifying feature—his facial hair. "The Beard," as many called him, was a Saratoga local. Perhaps he loved the stage here too much to ever leave. Others think the theater's resident spirit is actor and director John Houseman. The theater was named after him for a while—why shouldn't he haunt it?

# The Shape-shifters of Saratoga

By now, you know that Saratoga is famous for its sparkling, healthy water. But the natural beauty of the area is well known, too. The lush green forests and hills around town are a refuge for wildlife. Don't be too sure, though, the sweet meadowlark you hear singing is really a bird. Or that the distant hooting you hear at nightfall is coming from an owl. You can never be too certain around here. What you're hearing might be a shape-shifter.

The indigenous people who lived in this area for centuries believed in spirits and fairies, but they also believe in witchcraft. The local wizards and witches weren't the sort of sorcerers that you might be thinking about. They didn't go to magic school, and they didn't ride broomsticks. They didn't wear pointy hats. Just like the water spirits, they had power over nature. In the local language, the name for a sorcerer translates to "power person." Unlike innocent water spirits, shape-shifters harness the power of nature for sinister purposes. Most indigenous groups believed that the witches and wizards in their communities had learned their wicked ways from rival nations. Surely none of their own people would use nature to do evil!

Mostly, witches and wizards in local legends liked to get revenge on others. One of the sneakiest ways to do it was to turn themselves into animals and spy on their enemies. They really liked to transform into birds because flying was a helpful power. But they were also known to turn into wolves, pigs, or even goats. The important thing to remember, legends cautioned, was that even though witches or wizards could look like animals, they still had their very sharp sorcerer's wits. They could think and plot and plan (and maybe even talk) just as well as they could when they were in their human forms.

So how do you know if the animal you encounter around town is a shape-shifting witch or wizard? Well, in old stories, the Abenaki said there might be a few tell-tale signs. For example, if you see a deer walking on its hind legs, this may actually be a sorcerer. Witches and wizards will often get their animals mixed up when they are shifting. So, for example, you might see an animal with a bear head, rabbit paws, a woodchuck body, and squirrel posture! This is almost certainly an enchanted, or "witched," animal.

Some legends say that there is another giveaway. One part of the sorcerer will always stay in its previous shape. Even if the sorcerer is in human form, it might have a foxtail, for example. If you encounter one of these shape-shifters, Abenaki legend advises, you should run as fast as you can in the opposite direction.

In one story from the Abenaki tradition, a hunter is in the woods and shoots an animal with his bow. The animal is struck and struggles off into the forest, leaving a bloody track. When the hunter follows the track, it leads to a cabin in the woods. Inside the cabin, there is a person with suspiciously similar wounds. Yep, it's a witch.

The Mohawk people also believed in shape-shifters.

A Mohawk woman who lives in the area recently told this spooky story that happened just a few years ago.

One night, she heard a commotion out in her pastures and went out to see what could be bothering her horses. When she got there, she saw that the horses had gathered on one side of the field. They were looking off in the direction of the fence. Against the fence, there were two dogs standing on their hind legs. It looked like they were having a serious conversation. They were leaning toward each other with their snouts almost touching and their ears cocked. They looked at the horses and then back to each other as if they had some decision to make. As the woman got closer, the dogs appeared to have seen her. She was close enough to hear them, and she swore one of them muttered something to the other in a language that she couldn't quite understand. Then the dogs dropped to all fours and acted like they were just regular dogs. They wagged their tails and approached her happily as if to greet her. She decided to just let them live with her. Ever since then, she has often thought that they might be carrying on conversations when she is not in the room, although she has not caught them at it again.

So, if you see an animal behaving strangely, take a moment to pause. You may have just had an encounter with a shape-shifter!

The Onondaga people believed that witches would meet in the middle of the forest at midnight to transform into their animal identities. How do you know if you've met a witch on the way to a meeting? They say there is a way, but it typically is only possible if you encounter one on an autumn or winter evening. You know how you can see your breath when you're outside on such a night? Well, a witch's or wizard's breath has a glow to it when it comes out, especially if he or she is coughing. That's because they have fire in their lungs. Their nose and mouth might glow a little bit red, too. If you see that, again, it's best to just run in the other direction.

If you do have an unpleasant encounter with a witch, there are people who can help. The medicine people of the area could redirect the dark forces of nature toward the light. They were good at finding out the source of a curse and prescribing a cure. But hopefully, for you, it won't come to that.

# Watch for the Witch Lights

The hour just before and after sunset is one of the spookiest times of day in Saratoga Springs. That's the time of day when you have a good chance of seeing one of Saratoga's best-known supernatural displays—the witch lights. Mysterious orbs of light are so common here, just about everyone has seen them. There's a good chance you will, too, if you know where to look.

It's well known in ghost hunting circles

that anomalous light phenomena (ALP in ghost-hunter lingo) are very common in haunted places. They can take different shapes, appear in different colors, and move at different speeds. But they always indicate one thing: a spirit is present. The reason a spirit appears in light form remains a mystery.

The Iroquois people called these orbs "witch lights." They believed they were the "astral form" of witches or possibly messengers sent by witches. When you think about it, that really would be a great way to move about undetected!

There are so many places you can see witch lights in Saratoga. There are many reported sightings at the Saratoga National Battlefield in Schuylerville. You can also see them at the Sacandaga Reservoir, the Devil's Den to the north of the village of Saratoga Springs, or in Bear Swamp. In local lore, these lights have been known to shoot out of the chimneys of people suspected of being witches or wizards. The lights hover across the sky and come to rest in a graveyard or a swamp before taking the shape of a sorcerer. That actually might be a little too scary to witness!

Witch lights come in all shapes, sizes, and colors, from pale white to fire-orange or red. For the Abenaki people, only the green lights were believed to be related to witches. Some glowing orbs seen around town are quite small, reported to be the size of baseballs. Others have been described as measuring the same size as a human head. Some move smoothly, and others have a herky-jerky motion.

Witnesses around Saratoga sometimes report a single glowing light streaking just above the tree line. Other times, there might be dozens of lights clustered together zipping around. It's almost as if the lights are playing pranks on the observers. In fact, some local families have fun trying to play tag with them when they appear in the forest, chasing them and trying to catch them! One boy followed a light to the base of a tree where it stopped and stood very still. Before the light faded out, he said he saw a group of tiny people in its glow. So, it's possible that the lights are actually associated with the fairies rather than the witches. Or maybe both types of supernatural beings control the mysterious lights.

In Iroquoian tradition, there's a story of a fur trapper encountering a mysterious floating light. The trapper was traveling through a swamp when he saw the light. He stood still, barely daring to breathe. A man emerged from the shadows. The trapper knew of a man the locals considered suspicious. They believed he was a wizard but could this man before the trapper be him? The wizard followed the light until it stopped, hovering in place. Then he stooped down and began to dig around in the muck, pulling something out and stuffing it under his cloak. The wizard crept back out of the shadows, and the light faded out. In another version of this story, the trapper watches the lights from the shadows of the trees. As one gets close to him, he sees the face of a witch inside it.

Don't be afraid of the mysterious glowing orbs, though. If you see one, it might just be the spirit of a recently departed person who has gotten lost or confused on the way to his or her final resting spot. That's what the Abenaki people believed. You could tell that a light was a lost soul instead of a witch if it was very pale. In Abenaki tradition, the lights would move along the horizon, searching for a herd of deer. The deer would help the soul to reach the "realm of the blessed." In particular, the souls needed to find a big buck deer with broad-spreading antlers. The buck would catch the ball of light in its antlers and bounce it up into the heavens. Deer were even known to collect these lights, basically herding them together so they could move on into the afterlife. This became a problem in modern times because the deer would see bouncing lights and try to help them, only to find that they were actually the headlights of cars. This led to some awful collisions and an unhappy end for the helpful deer.

A local storyteller said that during the Great Depression, when a flu epidemic hit the area particularly hard, his grandfather passed away. Yet just hours before, his young cousin had also been taken by the illness. Looking out the window shortly after the grandfather died, a family member noticed a small pale ball of light moving uncertainly through the yard. It hovered close to the house as if it wanted to enter. Moments later, a powerful glowing orb appeared. The two orbs circled each other as if they were happily dancing and embracing each other. In fact, one family member said the smaller, paler orb seemed like an excited puppy. The glow from the small orb became stronger, and the movements of the lights smoothed out. The two balls of light floated off together into the trees. Even in their grief, the family felt relieved. The soul of the grandson had joined with the grandfather who knew its way off into the realm of the blessed.

Saratoga National Historic Park

# Battlefield Ghosts

It's quiet and peaceful now, but for hundreds of years, Saratoga was the scene of quite a few bloody battles. Many different nations clashed with each other here. The Mohawk and the Adirondack fought. The French and the Iroquois fought. The Algonquin and the Iroquois fought. The British and the French fought. And then, of course, the British fought the American colonists. So, it's not surprising that a lot of ghost soldiers stayed put here in the place where they took their last breath.

There were so many battles fought here, so long ago that only a historian would know the location of all the battlegrounds. But some say you can feel a certain spooky energy in these places, even if there is no indication of what took place there. For example, hundreds of years ago along the Mourning Kill River near Ballston (just south of Saratoga), the Mohawk and the Adirondack had a terrible skirmish. In that spot now, strawberries grow, a symbol, some say, of the blood that was spilled there. This is another spot where mysterious lights have been seen.

There's a well-known story about the Battle of Stiles Tavern, a place where the

British and French took up arms in 1693. A tavern was later built on the site. Years went by, and it became a private home—a very haunted private home. Phantom dancers were seen spinning around the floors to the faint sound of music. Lights flickered. Appliances turned themselves on and off. Buttons would appear out of nowhere. A ghost girl in old-fashioned clothes was seen in one of the windows. Outside, a legless ghost wandered, searching the nearby bushes. Could he be one of the stricken soldiers, looking for his legs?

One battle that is very well known is the Battle of Saratoga, one of the most important battles of the Revolutionary War. It took place here in 1777. The month-long battle was one of the first major victories for the Americans. They weren't professional soldiers. Most of them were farmers and blacksmiths. But the battle showed that the Continentals—as the Americans were called—might really be underestimated. They might just stand a chance against the Red Coats, the best-trained army in the world at the time.

The leader of the British forces was General Burgoyne, also known as Gentleman Johnny. He was an aristocrat who was said to have arrived at the battle with thirty wagonloads of personal items. He was counting on help from reinforcements to help him win the battle. But due to some communications errors, they never arrived. Instead, battles raged for a month all around the Saratoga area. Burgoyne surrendered, but not before many lives were lost on both sides.

The Battle of Saratoga was not contained in one location. There are sites where there were hospitals and burial grounds. There are sites of small skirmishes outside the main battlefields. So, it's not surprising that the ghosts are spread out all over the area! The first place you might meet them, though, is in Saratoga National Historical Park.

One boundary of the park runs along Route 4.

If you are really focused on seeing a ghost soldier, you may want to head there. It runs along the Hudson River. Through the years, many tourists and travelers have seen ghosts along this road, near the river. The time of day or year doesn't matter. Ghosts have been spotted there in broad daylight, in the middle of the summer. In fact, some motorists have reported driving right through them on a misty, steamy day! Panicked drivers have stopped their cars and run back to the scene of what they believed to be an accident, only to find nothing there. One witness reported seeing a German battalion moving along Route 4. Cars slammed right through the troops unaware. The troops, it seems, were equally unaware of the cars. Usually, you won't spot a whole ghost army. But you might see a single ghost or a small company of soldiers.

Jon Neilson Farmhouse, Saratoga National Historic Park

You may be surprised to learn that the ghost soldiers aren't always engaged in a fight. There are frequent reports of horse and rider apparitions. Could they be scouts on the way to deliver some important battle position intelligence to their commanders? Sometimes, ghosts are seen running and walking, clad in their battle uniforms. Only the most experienced historians can tell exactly which army the soldier belongs to. Unless they are wearing red coats, that is. Those are certainly easy to spot!

One of the most famous soldiers to haunt the battlefield is British commander Simon Fraser. The story goes that Fraser was shot down from a distance by a Continental sharpshooter. Fraser fell from his horse, hit in the midsection. The men under his command carried him to a nearby house. The wife of one of the German soldiers in his battalion tended to him. But it was too late, and he passed away. He was buried that evening on a hill that had been turned into a makeshift fort. Although it's not clear now where this grave is actually located, there is a monument to him in the park.

You may not be surprised to learn that the mysterious witch lights often seen around Saratoga have also been spotted around Fraser's monument. They are said to be green. Some believe they might be a manifestation of his ghost. But there's another possible explanation. They might be witches or their emissaries. Surely, a battlefield is a place where someone with wicked intentions might have worked some black magic.

The hauntings at former battlefields aren't always apparitions. Sometimes, visitors report hearing ghostly conversations. One group of battle re-enactors were camping in the park when they heard the sudden onrush of horse hooves and the dragging of chains.

Urgent voices shouted commands they couldn't understand.

People who have been in the battlefield parking lot at night have reported a sudden gust of wind howling, as if the sound of a raging battle is being carried across the field. In the wind, they hear the screams and cries of anguished soldiers, the clash of steel, and the echo of musket fire. Some have even said they have had the sense that a conversation is taking place, although they can't make out the words or the accents. A pair of park rangers heard one such conversation on the night of the anniversary of the battle of Bemis Heights. They tried to record the sound, but no one was able to distinguish exactly what was being said. If you really want to know what happened on the battlefield, though, you might do well to stop at the park's visitor center. There is a lot of great information there about the battle and those who took part in it!

# The Ghosts of Broadway

It's a lively shopping street running straight through downtown Saratoga Springs. But is Broadway also the most haunted street in town? Most definitely! Almost every building on the street is connected to supernatural happenings. You know that Saratoga's springs are filled with spirit energy. But did you know that many of Broadway's buildings are built on top of springs? Perhaps some of the spirit energy just had to have somewhere to go. Or maybe there are other explanations. Let's take a look at some of the Broadway hauntings to try to find out.

On the 300 block of Broadway, you'll find the grand and very haunted Adelphi hotel, built in 1873. If you happen to be a guest here, don't let that scare you. There's a ghost there that's said to be harmless or perhaps helpful. This spirit once took all the lightbulbs out of the second-floor ceiling fixtures and piled them on a hall table. It sometimes shows up in photographs, a spectral presence in an otherwise empty room. One photographer, however, believes that the haunting here might be the work of more than one spirit. In a photograph she took, the image revealed a shadowy disembodied leg here, a head there. Had the camera caught bits and pieces of many different ghosts? There's only one spirit in the building that might give you a fright. A woman dressed in nineteenth-century clothing has been spotted in the basement. Her face is said to be terrifying. Some speculate she is the ghost of someone who perished in a fire. The story frightened some employees so much that they refuse to go into this area of the hotel.

Continuing down Broadway, you'll come to the Arcade, the scene of a terrible fire in 1902. This imposing building is home to several businesses. It is known to include several underground tunnels that offer access to neighboring structures. Some say the supernatural things that happen here might be connected to the spirits of those who perished here long ago.

Looking in the window of one of the street-level businesses, witnesses have sometimes seen shadowy figures, undetected by those working there. The sound system has been known to turn on by itself. A photographer who works in the building saw a ghost in the doorway of his studio. Another time, he saw a man in old-timey clothing. When he spoke to the man, the man turned and disappeared right through a brick wall! Objects in the photographer's studio have moved on their own. When the photographer appeals to the unseen presence to return a lost item, it is quickly returned to its place.

In the awful fire of 1902, several people and several cats lost their lives. People who work in the building now report that they will feel something brush against their leg but discover that nothing is there. Have they just had an encounter with a ghost cat?

Moving down Broadway, you'll come to the Algonquin, an impressive apartment building

designed in 1892 for a local carriage maker and housewares salesman. Those who live here say it's just buzzing with supernatural energy. Like other places in Saratoga, mysterious lights have been seen here, hovering over the building. Some believe the spirit of an old elevator operator haunts the building—the elevators sometimes go up and down on their own or stop at random floors for no reason!

Another ghost that's sometimes spotted here has been described as a well-dressed woman. Sometimes the hem of her long gown will appear under a door before being whisked away.

The building has an unusual design, with some apartment windows actually opening to an indoor space. Here, residents say, there is a

curious whispering sound sometimes. There's also a windowless hall that is said to have been built so that the dead and dying could be taken out of the building without being seen. Residents report hearing strange bumps in this hall.

Strangely, this is the second building on Broadway that is said to have a ghost cat!

Continuing down Broadway, you'll notice a welcoming and distinctive storefront with an arched entry, big glass windows, and an old-fashioned tile floor. The worn wooden door looks like it has welcomed many guests through the years. And it has. For many years, this building was home to a restaurant and bar called Professor Moriarty's. The bar was named after the mysterious villain in the Sherlock Holmes stories, so maybe it's not surprising that the place is haunted. The author of the Sherlock Holmes stories, Sir Arthur Conan Doyle, was famous for believing in spiritualism, the ability to talk to those who had passed on to the other side of the grave. Could that be the reason that one or more spirits chose to haunt this place?

Professor Moriarty's was in operation for over 20 years. During that time, many of the staff members at "Professor's" (as locals called it) reported a kind of supernatural energy in the place. But after some time, they realized that it was haunted by at least one very specific ghost—a former Saratoga resident named Malcolm. Malcolm lived in Saratoga Springs his whole life. A veteran of World War II, he worked as a postman and later a post office superintendent. When he retired, he ended up feeling bored. Although he had plenty of money, he wanted to get back to work. He took a job as a janitor and helper at the restaurant. He was the person who would stay around after closing time to get everything cleaned up. He was a very popular member of the staff, loved by co-workers and patrons alike. He had wild, long white hair and a beard. He drove around in a stylish convertible car. He loved to dance. People said he especially liked reggae music. Put on a Bob Marley song, and you couldn't get him off the dance floor!

On the days he worked, Malcolm would get to Professor's early and enjoy himself before his night cleaning job started. If he was tired, he'd take a nap in a certain area of the kitchen. When the restaurant finally closed, he'd work as long as it took to clean the restaurant. Malcolm told some of his co-workers that he wasn't lonely at night. While he was working, he'd talked to the spirits that inhabited the restaurant.

One morning in 1992, the restaurant owner came in to find Malcolm slumped over one of the tables. He had died during the night. But according to those who've spent time in the place, he never really left.

When reggae music is played in the restaurant, some people reported seeing a wispy apparition swaying along to the music. Some say that Malcolm actually brought along some of the other spirits who inhabit the place to dance with him!

After Professor's closed, a different restaurant opened and there is still one there today. While some things may have changed, since the time of Professor Moriarty's, one thing is definitely the same. Malcolm has stayed put. The staff said that he enjoys playing pranks, such as moving picture frames just slightly, messing with the lights, or flushing the bathroom toilets when no one is inside. Sometimes, he tips over drinks. The restaurant has old-fashioned lights that can be turned on and off with a chain that hangs from the fixture. People who knew him when he was alive say that Malcolm liked to use a pair of ice tongs to grab and pull the chains and shut off the lights. Now, as a ghost, he manages to keep doing it, although no one knows how. Sometimes, staff will hear his

footsteps at night. Perhaps he's still too bored to stop working and is back at his old job.

If you're on Broadway, why not stop by to see if you can sense Malcolm's presence?

Last, but not least, you may not be surprised to learn that the town's historic firehouse, built in 1884, is most certainly haunted. It hasn't been used as a firehouse in many years. Recently, the building has housed a restaurant and other businesses. But some believe those early firefighters were so dedicated to their jobs that they never left. In the place where the fire pole used to be, some business owners and employees have seen a shimmering light, as if light is reflecting off a metallic surface that's no longer there. Some have reported seeing "extra" figures coming down the stairs along with parties of diners. Perhaps surprisingly, no one has ever reported hearing a phantom fire alarm here.

# The Haunted Hotel

Tourists have been coming to Saratoga Springs for centuries. So, it's not surprising that one of the area's oldest hotels is haunted. Perhaps some of the many people who've passed through the area have loved it so much they wanted to stay forever? It's certainly possible.

Even before the Revolutionary War, the little log cabin that sat on what's now Maple Street was an inn. During the War, it expanded to include a tavern. A blacksmith shop was set up on the site. The owner of this establishment was a friendly fellow named Alexander Bryan. He welcomed both British and Americans. Through his friendship with the soldiers of the British army, he discovered that there was an upcoming battle. He rushed to the Americans to share information that would help them. After the war, his son opened a stone inn on the site of his father's old log cabin.

The hotel is now called the Olde Bryan Inn. It's operated as a restaurant. But are the former inn guests still here? Almost certainly. Through the years, many have reported seeing a Revolutionary soldier in the dining room. If you need to use the restroom when you are there, you might want to wait until after you leave. It can get pretty crowded in the second-floor bathroom. A colonial-era man and his horse have been seen there. What's more, the man is carrying a lance, a sword-like weapon that

was common hundreds of years ago. Historians say that such a weapon would not have been uncommon during the Revolutionary War. Soldiers on both sides of the conflict used a weapon called spontoon, which is basically like a spear with a very decorative head on the end. Hopefully, you will not have to defend yourself if you find it necessary to use the restroom!

Other visitors to the Olde Bryan have seen a ghost woman dressed in green. She has been one of the most constant apparitions in the inn, and people call her Eleanor. Some say that, more often than not, she's seen by children because they have stronger psychic powers than adults. One of the restaurant's servers reported that a child who was eating here with her grandmother refused to climb the stairs. She told her grandmother that she could see the ghost standing at the top. No one else could see anything. The lady in green is often seen floating in the restaurant's dining room, heading upward. It could be because there used to be a staircase in that very spot!

When it wasn't being used as an inn or restaurant, the stone structure was a family home for many decades. A member of the family that lived there believes that the woman in green is Beatrice Veitch. She had a green dress like the one the ghost is said to wear. But that might not be correct. The woman in green was seen when Beatrice was still alive! People have also reported feeling a light touch on their arms. It's a kind touch, but still, it's alarming when you realize there's no one there with you!

In addition to the ghosts, there have been reports of other supernatural happenings at the

Olde Bryan Inn. The face of an old woman will appear in a mirror from time to time. If you are looking in the mirror, she will be standing behind you. Spooky! Those who work here have also reported very common supernatural phenomena: lights turning on and off by themselves. A chandelier sways strangely on its own when there is no draught in the room. Sure, it could just be the quirks of a very old building. But it might be that some of Saratoga's longest-staying tourists are reaching out to welcome you.

# CHAPTER 7

# Spooky Mansions

Saratoga Springs was one of the fanciest places to live on the East Coast in the late 1800s, the period called the Gilded Age. Wealthy people came here and built mansions, some of them just as vacation homes! If you drive around town, you'll see so many of these grand homes, just as splendid as they were in the past. The late nineteenth century was a thrilling time to live here. Perhaps that's why many of the former residents of these mansions still haunt them today.

Take the magnificent Batcheller Mansion, with its many towers and cupola. It was built in 1873 for the Batcheller family. It is so large and expensive to upkeep that it was abandoned for many years. It served as a retirement home for some time and also as a hotel. Now, it's a bed-and-breakfast inn. Even before it became an inn, there were reports of strange happenings at the mansion. Footsteps in the halls when no one was there. Flickering lights, cold drafts of air. The scent of perfume or cologne wafting through a room for no reason. Now that there are guests regularly staying in the mansion, some have reported seeing the wispy form of a man in Victorian clothing in the dining room. Others say they've experienced the unsettling feeling that they are being watched.

Could the watcher be the former mistress of the house, Catharine Batcheller? She certainly had reason to want to stay here. If you visit the Saratoga Springs Historical Society, you'll see an emerald-green dress she wore to one of her famous balls in 1890. It cost $5,000, which, at the time, was more than most people made in a year. Perhaps Catherine had such a great time at the party that she never wanted it to end.

If the Batcheller Mansion is not spooky enough for you, there's an even spookier house located at 108 Circular Street. With its tall Greek columns running to the roof, it just looks like it might be haunted. Built in 1843 for millionaire James Savage, it's often still called the Savage House, but it's also been called the Isbell House, after a family who occupied it later. The grand structure has been used for many different things through the years, including an apartment building, a boardinghouse, a performing arts center, and several different times, a hotel. It has also been unoccupied at times—at least by living people.

Some say it was during the 1920s and 1930s

that the house was at its liveliest. That's when the Isbell family lived here. They had many important guests, including opera singers from New York City and the most famous movie stars of the era. When the fortunes of the house declined, and it became an apartment building, something terrible is said to have happened here.

The story goes that a man killed his wife's boyfriend on the second floor of the mansion. Decades later, it's said, a gun and a bloody rag were found in a hidey-hole in the house. Now, the spirit of the slain lover is said to walk the floor with heavy footsteps. Doors have been known to slam when no one is around. Furniture has been said to move on its own. Of course, this leads to speculation. Could the man who was murdered here live on as a spirit?

The murder may explain the second-floor ghost, but what about the ghostly birds? People have reported apparitions of red birds inside the house. They can even hear the ghost birds chatter!

It could be because the former owner Elisha Isbell kept an aviary in the house. According to local stories, a whole flock of birds escaped their cages and fluttered through the house one night. Were all the birds ever really caught or do they still haunt the home today?

There seems to be no explanation for why the iron fence outside the home is hot to the touch even when it is cold out and even after the sun goes down.

There's also quite an interesting story that took place during the period when the house was unoccupied. A group of high school drama students got permission to hold a costume party at the home. They were surprised that some older people they didn't know had joined the party. Who invited them? The uninvited guests spoke among themselves but didn't really interact with the students. The whole thing seemed strange. It was only a few days later when they realized just how strange it had really been. They realized that those uninvited guests had been ghosts.

It's not just the drama students who attract ghosts in Saratoga's haunted mansions. Writers do, too. One of the most famous artists' and writers' retreats in America is located here on an old estate once owned by the wealthy Trask family. The retreat is called Yaddo. Creative people are known to have active imaginations. But is it just imagination that accounts for the many ghost sightings here? One author who stayed here said that some of his fellow residents had seen a dark-haired woman and a soldier in a red coat arguing near the lake on the edge of the estate. They were most certainly phantoms from the Revolutionary War period, the witness said. A writer who was staying at the retreat said that the ghost of a Victorian woman appeared in his room. Now that's inspiration for a good story. He's not the only one who saw a Victorian woman on the grounds, though. Others report a "woman in white" apparition that some believe is the home's original owner, Katrina Trask.

Was it just an overactive imagination that caused one writer in the 1930s to report the sighting of a very famous ghost here? He said he saw the ghost of author Edgar Allen Poe walking the grounds and even heard him speak a few lines of his most famous poem, "The Raven." Whether or not it is true, it certainly makes a good story!

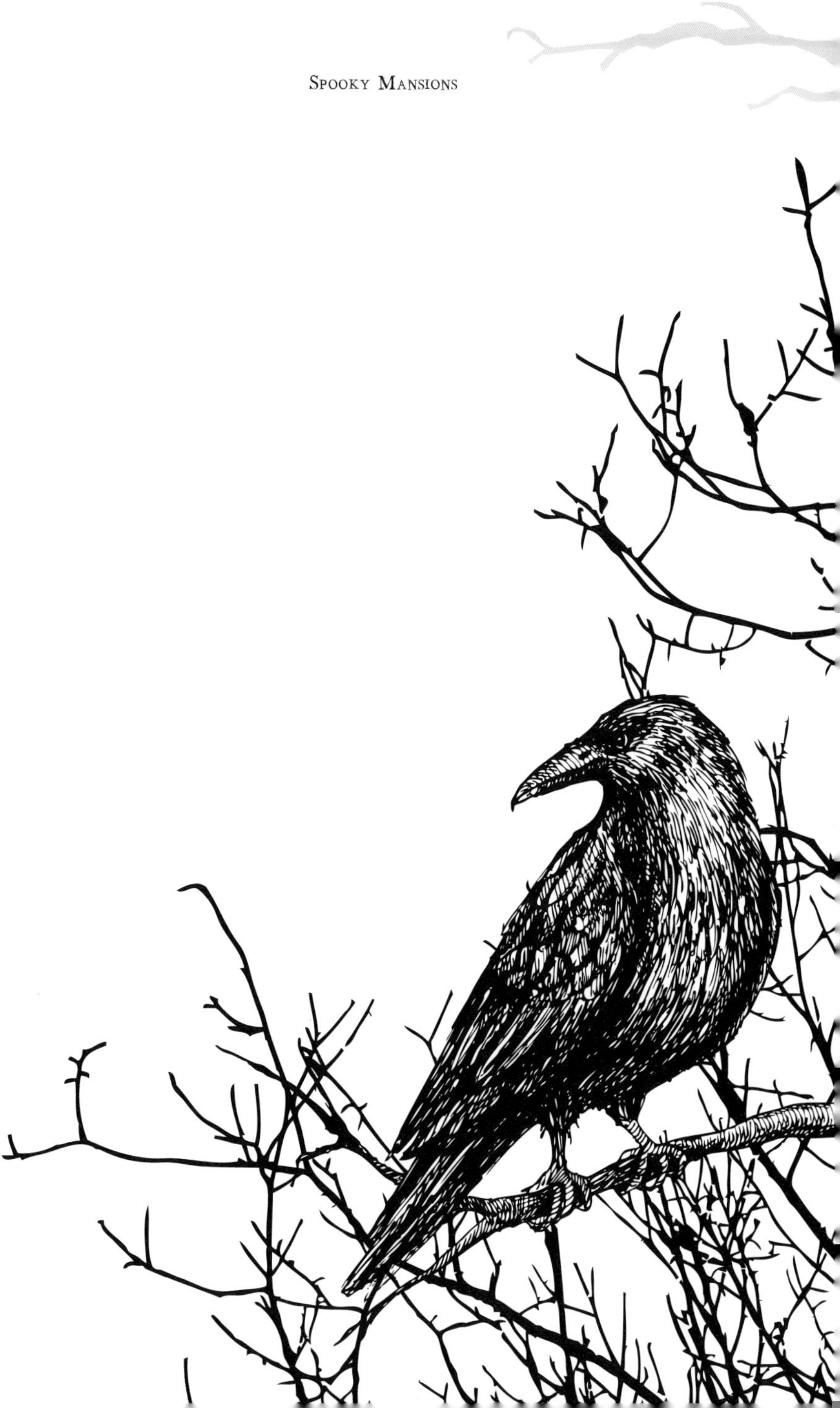

Canfield Casino Museum

# CHAPTER 8

# The Ghosts of the Casino

One of the must-do tourist activities in Saratoga is a walk through Congress Park. It's a beautiful place with walking paths, statues, pools, and streams. There's even an old carousel! Within the grounds of the park, you'll find the Canfield Casino, once a popular gambling spot. These days, the beautiful old building is used for weddings and special events. There's even a museum housed in the former casino—the

Saratoga Springs History Museum. The building was originally a "clubhouse" built by the famous boxer John Morrissey, who had the nickname "Old Smoke." He was so successful in the ring that he made a fortune. He was said to be a very snappy dresser, often seen wearing a diamond pin in his necktie. After he died, the clubhouse became a casino during Saratoga's heyday in the 1890s. Wealthy visitors came from all over to try their luck here. Gambling became illegal in New York decades later. Then the casino became a museum. Those who have worked here through the years believe that Old Smoke still lingers in the place where he spent his final years.

One spooky story took place at the museum in the 1990s. Three visiting children raced ahead of their parents, reaching the second floor without them. A few minutes later, one of the siblings came running back to a museum attendant. There was a scary old man upstairs, she said. But there was no one upstairs at the time. This is far from the only report of a haunting at the former casino. There is an old roulette wheel here that was left behind after the gambling operation closed. The staff has reported that it will begin to spin on its own when no one is around. What a creepy sight and sound that must be!

A security guard who was working at the museum one night got quite a scare as he made his rounds. He had heard the rumors of the hauntings here, so he brought an extra flashlight along. He made sure that both flashlights were charged. As he walked the upper floors, they both cut out, and he was left in complete darkness. He used his hands to feel his way back down the stairs, all the while sensing that he was being watched. When he got back down the stairs, both flashlights began to work again. He never returned to the job after that night.

Some say that a faint whiff of cigar smoke can be detected at times on the upper floor. Morrissey, the original owner of the building, was known to love smoking cigars. Could it be that Old Smoke is present, engaging in one of his favorite pastimes?

Believe it or not, he's not the only well-known ghost at the museum. In the museum's collection, there are several objects that once belonged to the Walworth family. They were a famous and wealthy family that had a long history dating back to the early days of Saratoga. At one time, they lived in a 55-room mansion on Broadway. There was a lot of drama in the family. One sister lost her fiancé in a shipwreck. One brother shot his father, who was said to be a terrible tyrant. But Reubena Hyde Walworth (known as Ruby) put her family's tragedies behind her and became a nurse during the Spanish-American War. She died from typhoid fever, contracted from the patients she served. She was buried in Greenridge Cemetery.

The mansion she grew up in was torn down in the 1950s. Is that why she haunts the museum instead? Some say they have seen the ghost of a woman believed to be Ruby walking in the hallway of the upper floors. Why do people think this ghost is Ruby? Well, because the ghost is wearing one of Ruby's dresses that is on display in the museum! One visitor saw the dress displayed and fainted. She had seen a ghost wearing the same dress earlier in the day! Ruby means no harm. In fact, those who say they have seen her say that she appears to be unaware of their presence. She simply goes about her business, equally unaware that she is a ghost.

If you don't happen to catch one of the casino's famous ghosts when they are haunting, you may still be able to experience something spooky in Congress Park. You may not be surprised to learn that Saratoga's mysterious orbs of light have been seen here, too.

Schuyler House, home of General Philip Schuyler

# The Haunting of the Schuyler Home

Have you heard of the musical Hamilton? It's about Alexander Hamilton, a Revolutionary War hero who later became the first treasurer of the United States. A big part of the musical is about Hamilton's wife, Eliza Schuyler (pronounced sky-ler), and her sisters Angelica and Peggy. They were the children of Philip Schuyler. Philip had made a name for himself during the French and Indian War. He became a general and helped to plan the early parts of the American Revolution, even the Battle of Saratoga, although he wasn't in charge of it.

When the Schuyler girls were young, their family used to come on camping trips just outside Saratoga. They even had some very important guests come to visit them, including George Washington. Their father decided to build a home here. Today, it's called the General Philip Schuyler House. Would you be surprised to learn that it is haunted?

The Schuyler family had already been in America for a long time before the Revolutionary War. In fact, their family was among the first Dutch settlers to live in New York. They farmed the land and later became very wealthy. Because of their powerful position, their support of the Revolution was important.

One of the battles in 1777 took place next to the Schuyler house. The house was destroyed. The family built a new house. It came under

British control during the war. Although it's not certain, it's believed that the house served as a field hospital. Not all the patients here survived. That could explain why some have said they've seen ghostly soldiers here displaying ghastly wounds. Some have even seen operating tables surrounded by ghost doctors and medics!

The soldiers and medical officers aren't the only ones who haunt the Schuyler House, though. People who work there say that at night, they will sometimes smell cigar smoke when no one is smoking. Some have even seen a glow like the lit end of a cigar. The staff of the house believes this to be the ghost of a man named David who once worked and lived at the house. But he may not be the only former resident who has stayed around. The staff thinks there are other ghosts that like to play pranks. They turn the lights on and off at night when no one else is around. They bang on the walls.

Their footsteps can be heard in the hallways. There's even a ghost bully! Some of the staff say that they have been shoved by this ghost. When they have finished tidying up, some phantom presence comes along and messes things up again! Then again, there might be a ghost that likes to tidy. Some staff members have found that invisible hands have finished work that was meant for them to do! One of the ghosts has an odd quirk. There is an old newspaper on display in the house. No matter which page it is open to, the ghost comes along and insists on turning it back to a specific page. Perhaps the ghost wants modern-day people to know what happened on that day?

Because of its connection to history, you will definitely want to visit the General Philip Schuyler House when you are in the area. But perhaps you'd also like to check out these rumors of hauntings at the house. It sounds like your chances of a ghostly encounter are pretty high!

nostilla ... idictodius ... sit
vit auctam, hoctem sedet publis,
iosum esulinequam imisulinit,
nit, que niur hilla novenat note
pridendi pereis. Catquo eo viri,
facendam opos, sente re pertus

### ART AND ENTERTAIMENT

vit intrae nem omnitem. Mulum et dit publica ia nius, num aris, strum pes, quodis ia quam confes consulis. O tabessupio ta nonfecurnime perum sulabit videperuntia re, ute opteatio us, tandit; Cupie que videlius. morunini convo, ut gra non presendum dicae ex morturbit. Bonularbit forbit. Utus C. Larei tus oculemum cons Catum ius, strat vissa actero urs andis vilit sent? Nam menatiure in Etriptis ... n tos, publi perit,

Olia ... ovehe
Rommovexed atu concupionsum it dicae, quem pulum que publice ne qu resenat uscio, cri, Palibul confect atur pliceps, cernissus, scertero vastisse aceperfestiu sum.
Inatiu in tenim nestra consum perisquam di cons novisqu emenat. Fordio vilin vertiu vis sendum, senat.
Omnost omnotiam pul videm strurniu cul co patu quissedit; nosules esciis publis erficer cen nerecris, quamdio tam

erum ... a que ta re, sena, aet intret aperii am-

...DAY, APRIL ... 1957.

**PRICE 2d**

# BEST OFFER!

confex noccide natictatella qua maximil hintrit facchuscis. Sciesi tatalis iae pulis ingules tisulvid Cuperid dees nosti pul ta vilis, non intimil ienequi ditabist dem iu cienter fectastam entelic molus;

potam re tem demod audem num pri, sena, us es, consi iam is esta rei pestiam elabus compestrit, nit vehebat, nes haecren arivivi ssuus, C. Verrica; hocrio, millari silq... dit. Um sentiquonsus et;

# The Witch of Saratoga

Picture this scene: it's the 1820s. The village of Saratoga Springs has just been established. It's a small town, but it's growing. There's a town hall and even a hotel. Most of the town's 2,000-or-so residents know each other. And all of them know The Witch, that strange woman who lives in a cabin in the woods about a mile outside of town. There she is in her hooded red cloak, reading someone's fortune on the street corner as she often does. Yes, everyone knows who she is. But do they really know her?

Angeline Tubbs was said to have come to America from England as a teenager with Burgoyne's army. When the British were defeated, it's said that she was left behind with no way of getting back to her home country. There are rumors that she had been engaged to one of the soldiers in Burgoyne's regiment. Was he killed in

the Battle of Saratoga? Or did he leave Angeline behind? No one really knows.

In her youth, Angeline was said to have been beautiful. But the townspeople didn't know what to make of her. Her association with the British army couldn't have helped. People were suspicious of anyone loyal to the Crown. Some said there was an attempt to hang her for her sympathy for the British. Years later, they said her disfigured appearance was the lingering mark of that attempt on her life.

There seems to be some truth to the rumor that she dabbled in the occult. She was known to "read the cards," or tell fortunes based on tarot cards. Townspeople spied on her in her forest home. There was always an unusual number of cats and dogs lingering inside and outside the cabin. That started a rumor that these animals were her "familiars," animals that witches are said to keep to do their bidding. There was another rumor that she would stay alive as long as one of

her cats was alive. She lived until 1865. If some calculations are correct, she would have been 104 at the time. A cat that belonged to her lived another 39 years after that if local rumors are true. That would indeed be a magically long life.

Ever since Angeline's time, there have been reports of her ghost still haunting the place where she once lived. It's part of an area called "the Devil's Den" because of all its spooky happenings.

This spot is just north of the Village of Saratoga Springs, north of Maple and East Avenues. The area has such a strong connection to her that the hill running from Second Street down to Maple Street is called Angeline Hill. In the 1930s, a writer staying at the nearby Yaddo Artists' Colony said he saw the Witch of Saratoga howling into the stormy night. It could have been her. Or maybe it was just a writer's active imagination?

# The Devil and Nelly Jones

Back in the old days, there was not a lot to do at night in the area near Saratoga Springs, especially in the winter. People liked to pass the time by telling stories, some of them quite spooky. This is one of them.

A long time ago, back before there was even a train station in town, there was a man named George Jones who lived in the southern part of Saratoga County. His wife, Nellie, was a spirited woman, full of life. But the two of them didn't get along that well. Sadly, they fought all the time.

After a particularly nasty fight, George was walking in the woods, feeling down about

everything in life. He didn't know what to do. It had gotten so bad that he wondered how he could find a way out of it all. "Maybe I should just sell my soul to the Devil," he thought out loud. For whatever reason, he repeated this strange thought out loud again and then again. Just after he had said it for the third time, the Devil appeared in front of him. To George, he looked a lot like the local preacher—a man in a black suit with a white neck collar, a harsh expression on his face. "What do you want with me?" the Devil asked.

George was terrified, but he knew that he'd gotten himself into this, and now he had to get himself out. "I'll sell myself to you if you'll take my wife away for 10 years," he sputtered.

The Devil seemed satisfied with the bargain.

A few mornings later, he showed up at the couple's home. Nelly was doing laundry and really didn't have time to entertain visitors. She was polite but not too welcoming to the stern-faced stranger. "Yes?" she asked when she answered the door. "What can I do for you?"

"You can help me by coming quietly," said the Devil.

"I beg your pardon!" Nelly said. "You've got a lot of nerve. You come here to my home demanding that I come with you? Where do you get off?"

This was not the response the Devil had been expecting. Usually, people were afraid of him. As he stepped into the house, Nelly whirled around and grabbed some hot tongs from the fireplace. She swung one of them around and landed it right on top of the Devil's head before he could dive under the table.

The Devil did have some experience with this sort of thing, though. Coming out from the other side of the table, he was able to grab Nelly and carry her out the door. Still holding her, he jumped onto his powerful horse, ready to take her off to the underworld. They rode like the

wind, with sparks coming out of the tail of his fiendish horse. They rode through Bear Swamp and approached Saratoga Lake. Nelly saw Snake Hill in front of her, a place that in local legend was said to be cursed. People said it was a gateway to the underworld. At the same moment, she saw something that gave her a clue as to who this fearful stranger was. Legend has it that no matter how well dressed the Devil appears, there is something that gives away his appearance. As she sat in the back and him in the saddle, Nelly could see the Devil's pig-like tail poking out from a slit in the back of his pants. She knew that she had to act fast. It was now or never.

Nelly grabbed the tail and twisted it as hard as she could. The Devil shrieked and tried to turn around and grab her, but she twisted even harder. The horse went out of control. The Devil grabbed Nelly's leg and threw her off of the saddle. She flew into the air, but instead of falling to the ground, an angel's hand reached out and caught her and guided her into a haystack where she landed softly. Just as she looked up, she saw the Devil and his horse leaping into White Sulphur Springs and disappearing.

She was shaken but none the worse for wear. Nelly headed home on the road through Bear Swamp. When she got there, she found the home

empty. Her husband, George, never returned and was never seen again after that day. Perhaps the Devil collected him since he couldn't get his hands on Nelly. But he may have also just run off to a new place, frightened by the terrible deed he'd done. No one will ever know, but this is a story that's been told in the area for many a year.

Believe it or not, this isn't the only local story that relates to the Devil, or "Old Scratch," as some call him. There's a street in town called Devil's Lane. This spooky name comes from a legend about a man who once lived there. It was long before the Revolutionary War when a Scottish immigrant named Angus McDearmuid lived here. The story goes that during a terrible thunderstorm, his cow ran off. He went out to find her and had the sense that someone was looking at him. When he turned to look, there was a terrifying figure behind him. It had a pale face, fiery-red eyes, and a wide-brimmed hat, but it had pig legs and smelled like sulfur.

McDearmuid was sure it was the Devil. He ran and made it home alive, promising he would be a good man forevermore so that he never had to encounter that creature again. People in town started calling his street Devil's Lane, and to this

day, some say strange things happen here and it has a spooky feel to it.

It's not the only local area that bears the Devil's name. The Devil's Den is a wooded area outside town that many now enjoy as a hiking and mountain biking area. But in the past, it was known for the strange happenings in the woods. It was said to be impossible to walk in the woods without getting lost. According to the Abenaki who once lived in the area, it was because of the trickster spirit who lived here. Later, locals were warned to stay away because of the many witch lights seen here. It was also the scene of shape-shifter sightings. Today, the trails are well marked, and you should be able to enjoy the great outdoors here. You just might want to return to your car before nightfall.

Saratoga Spa State Park

# Conclusion

You are certainly going to have a good time during your visit to Saratoga Springs. You may have a wonderful day walking through one of the parks. You might stroll Broadway and stop in at a local restaurant for a memorable meal. You will probably go to Saratoga National Historical Park with your family to learn about this important part of the Revolutionary War. But make sure to stay alert for the harder-to-see local sights.

Keep your eyes trained on the horizon around sunset to try to catch some of the area's many mysterious lights. Watch the road for companies of ghost soldiers. Stay quiet for a few moments, listening for the sounds of a long-ago battle on the wind. If you pay attention, you may just get to experience Saratoga's spooky side. But don't be afraid. These supernatural spirits are just another part of the long and fascinating history of this beautiful part of the country. Consider yourself lucky to have an up-close and personal encounter with the past. Even if you don't connect with the spirits in person, now you've gotten to know them a little better through reading this book!

Saratoga Springs, New York

**Kate Byrne** grew up listening to Irish ghost stories and still can't resist reading and writing about haunted mansions, castles, and forests.

Check out some of the other Spooky America titles available now!

Spooky America was adapted from the creeptastic Haunted America series for adults. Haunted America explores historical haunts in cities and regions across America. Each book chronicles both the widely known and less-familiar history behind local ghosts and other unexplained mysteries. Here's more from *Supernatural Saratoga* author Mason Winfield:

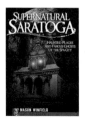